really easy piano

ABBA

Front cover photos courtesy of LFI

ISBN: 978-1-84449-569-6

For all works contained herein:
Unauthorized copying, arranging, adapting, recording, Internet posting, public performance,
or other distribution of the music in this publication is an infringement of copyright.
Infringers are liable under the law.

Visit Hal Leonard Online at
www.halleonard.com

Contact us:
Hal Leonard
7777 West Bluemound Road
Milwaukee, WI 53213
Email: info@halleonard.com

In Europe, contact:
Hal Leonard Europe Limited
Dettingen Way
Bury St Edmunds, Suffolk, IP33 3YB
Email: info@halleonardeurope.com

In Australia, contact:
Hal Leonard Australia PTY. Ltd.
4 Lentara Court
Cheltenham, Victoria, 3192 Australia
Email: info@halleonard.com.au

ANGELEYES	4
CHIQUITITA	6
DANCING QUEEN	8
THE DAY BEFORE YOU CAME	10
DOES YOUR MOTHER KNOW	12
FERNANDO	29
GIMME! GIMME! GIMME! (A MAN AFTER MIDNIGHT)	14
HEAD OVER HEELS	16
I DO, I DO, I DO, I DO, I DO	18
I HAVE A DREAM	20
KNOWING ME, KNOWING YOU	22
LAY ALL YOUR LOVE ON ME	24
MAMMA MIA	26
MONEY, MONEY, MONEY	28
THE NAME OF THE GAME	30
ONE OF US	32
RING RING	34
S.O.S.	36
SUMMER NIGHT CITY	38
SUPER TROUPER	39
TAKE A CHANCE ON ME	40
THANK YOU FOR THE MUSIC	42
VOULEZ-VOUS	48
WATERLOO	44
THE WINNER TAKES IT ALL	46

Angeleyes

Words & Music by Benny Andersson & Bjorn Ulvaeus

Recorded in 1978 (its first title, wisely abandoned, was 'Katakusom'). 'Angeleyes' was originally released as a double A-side along with 'Voulez-Vous', which received the most radio plays.

Hints & Tips: Play this song with an easy, relaxed feel. Notice that the opening eight bars are repeated. Play the bass line regularly and smooth.

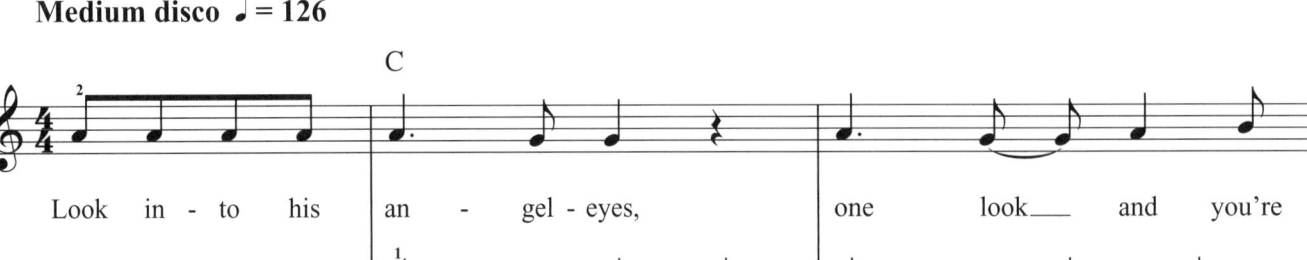

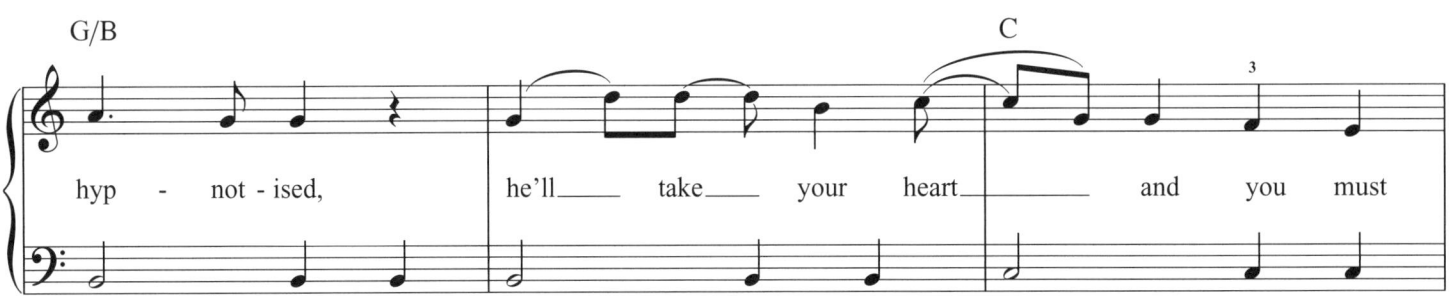

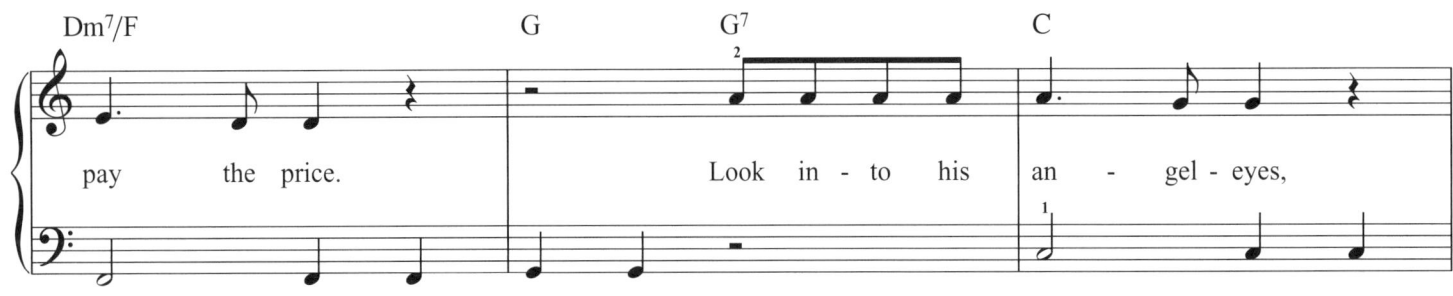

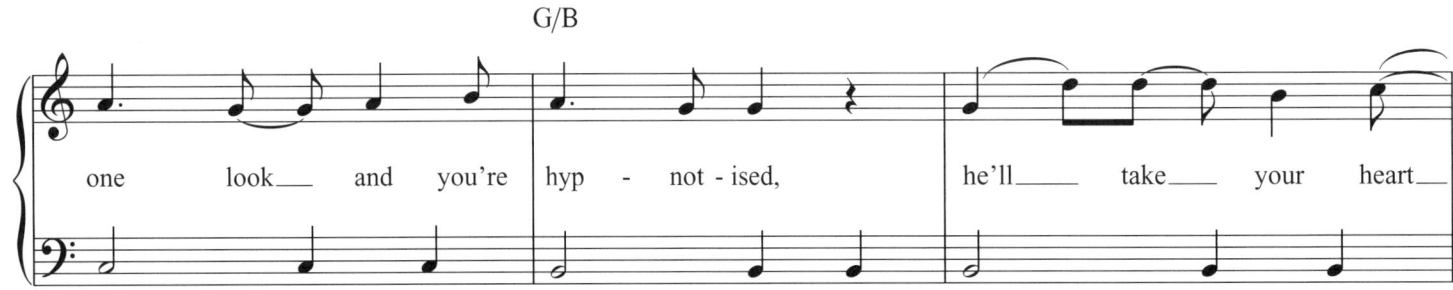

© Copyright 1979 Union Songs AB, Sweden. Bocu Music Limited for Great Britain and the Republic of Ireland.
All Rights Reserved. International Copyright Secured.

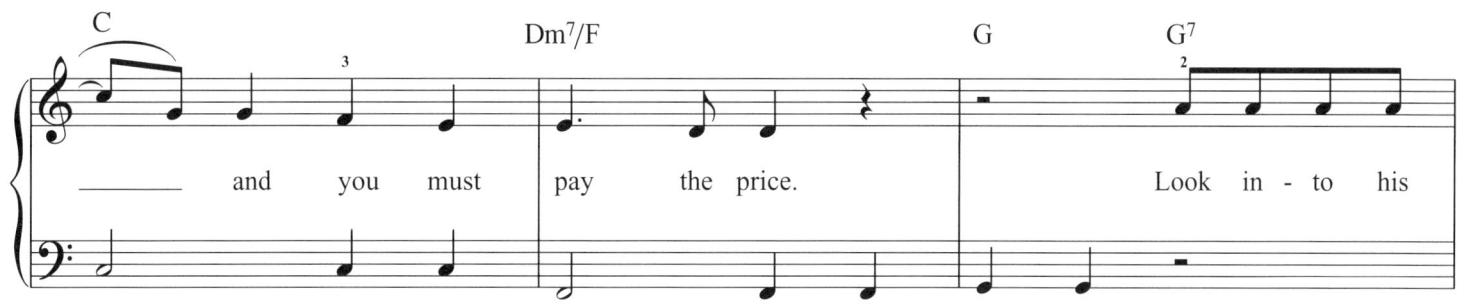
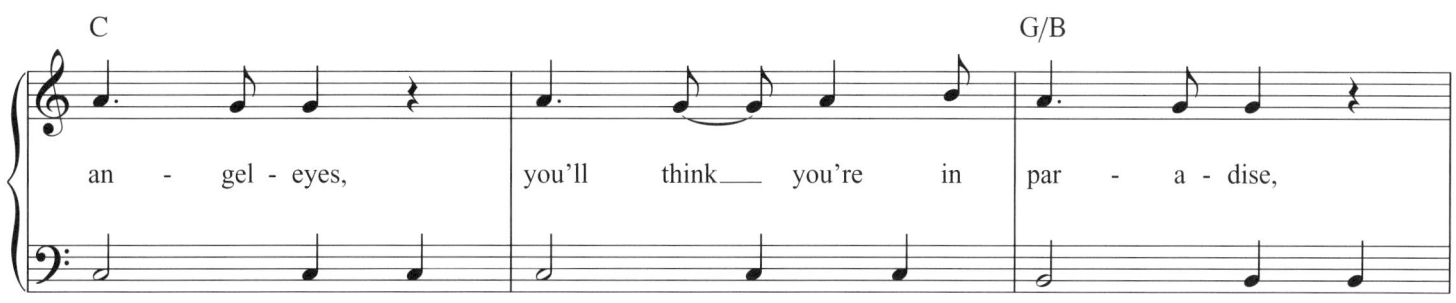
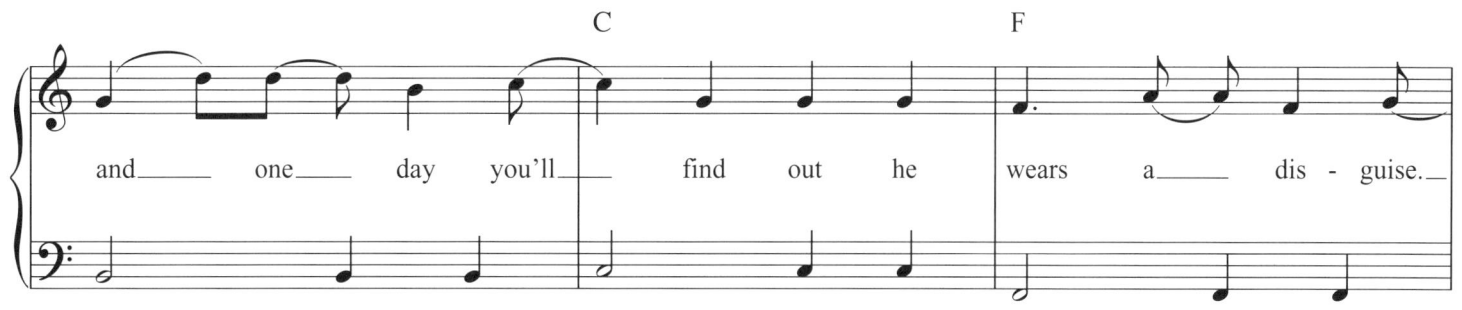
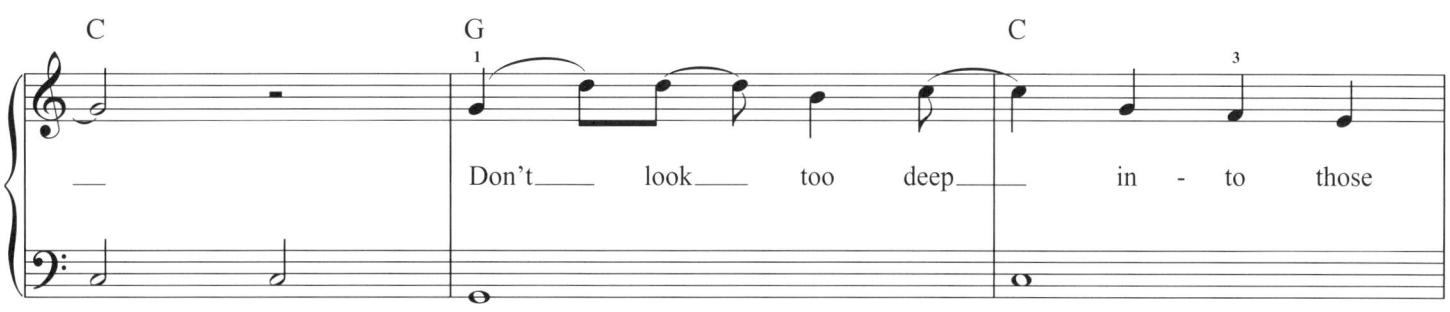

Chiquitita

Words & Music by Benny Andersson & Bjorn Ulvaeus

Abba's second Latin-flavoured hit (after 'Fernando') was chosen as a single release from the *Voulez-Vous* album instead of 'If It Wasn't For The Nights'. Its reward was to become Abba's fifth consecutive No.1 in Ireland.

Hints & Tips: Most of this piece has four counts to the bar – but some bars are made up of five counts and need special care. Don't miss the **rit.** (slow down) at the end of the piece.

© Copyright 1979 Music for UNICEF/Bocu Music Limited.
All Rights Reserved. International Copyright Secured.

Dancing Queen

Words & Music by Benny Andersson & Bjorn Ulvaeus & Stig Anderson

The ultimate disco song that finally made Abba big in the United States, was originally called 'Boogaloo'.
It was No.1 Stateside and almost everywhere else in 1976.
The drum part was inspired by George McCrae's 1974 disco hit 'Rock Your Baby'.

Hints & Tips: Take care with the rhythm of the melody. Say the words as you play, to help you, and practise slowly. Listening to the original recording may also help.

© Copyright 1976 Union Songs AB, Sweden. Bocu Music Limited for Great Britain and the Republic of Ireland.
All Rights Reserved. International Copyright Secured.

The Day Before You Came

Words & Music by Benny Andersson & Bjorn Ulvaeus

Abba's melancholy farewell masterpiece is unlike anything else they ever did. Except for a snare drum overdub, the backing track had nothing but Benny Andersson's synthesiser and a drum machine.
The lyric, a bleak diary chronicling a half-lived suburban life, was the best Abba ever wrote.

Hints & Tips: This song includes several changes of time – count carefully so that you get them right. Also, take care with the fingering of the first two notes of the melody.

© Copyright 1982 Union Songs AB, Sweden. Bocu Music Limited for Great Britain and the Republic of Ireland.
All Rights Reserved. International Copyright Secured.

Does Your Mother Know

Words & Music by Benny Andersson & Bjorn Ulvaeus

Originally a boogie rock number called 'I Can Do It', the first recorded version opened with a 30-second instrumental intro that was cut from the released track. After a number of other studio tweaks it triumphed as a thumping disco hit.

Hints & Tips: Don't miss the 2/4 bar near the beginning. To make this song even easier to learn, first practise it without the ties – that is, playing the tied notes.

© Copyright 1979 Union Songs AB, Sweden. Bocu Music Limited for Great Britain and the Republic of Ireland.
All Rights Reserved. International Copyright Secured.

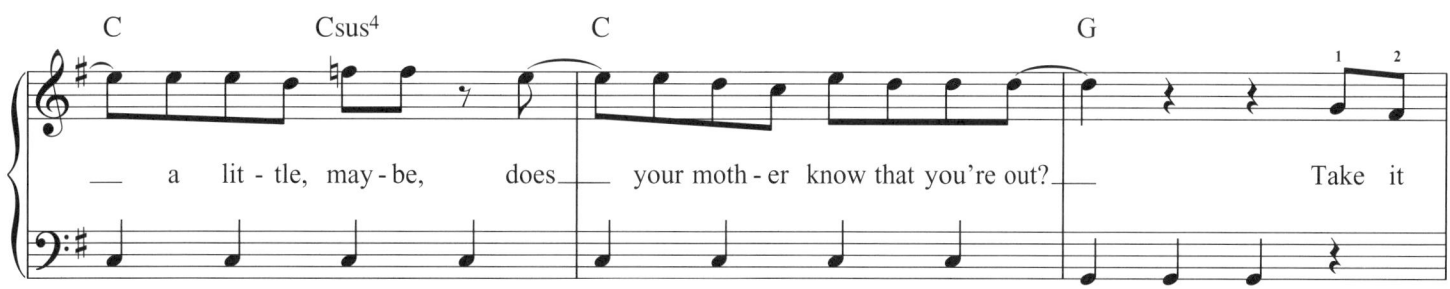

Gimme! Gimme! Gimme!
(A Man After Midnight)

Words & Music by Benny Andersson & Bjorn Ulvaeus

A durable Abba number which has been employed as a UK TV comedy theme song in addition to its first success as a 1979 chart hit in many European territories.

Hints & Tips: Always play 'half past twelve' and 'autumn winds' loudly, and then allow the repeated Gs in the bass to give the song its heavy beat feel.

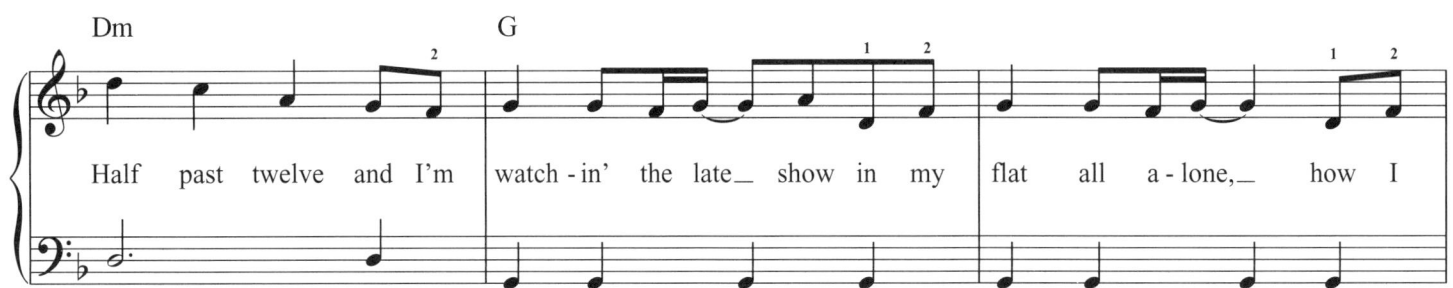

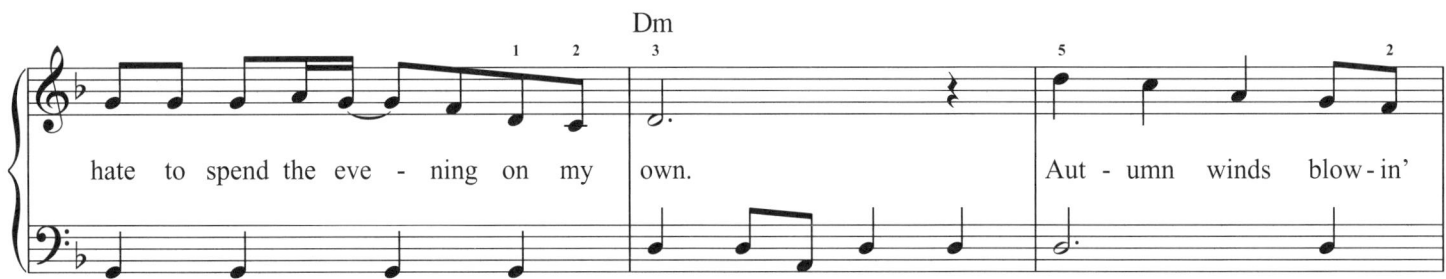

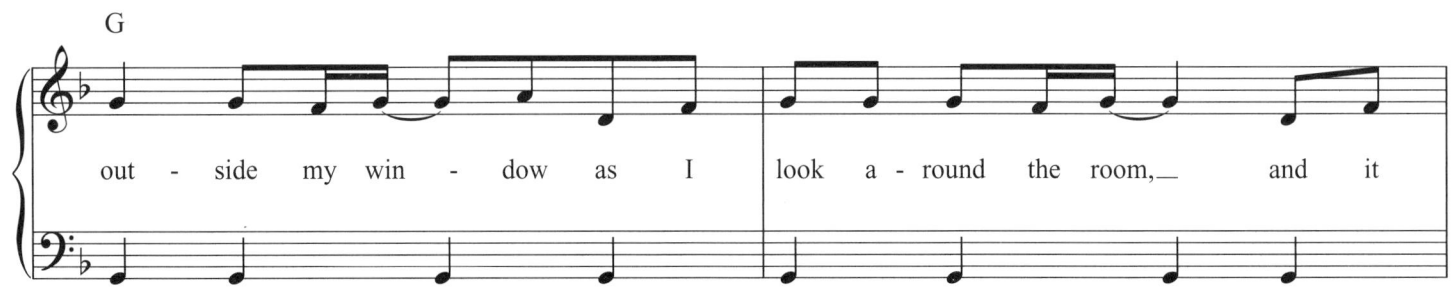

© Copyright 1979 Union Songs AB, Sweden. Bocu Music Limited for Great Britain and the Republic of Ireland.
All Rights Reserved. International Copyright Secured.

Head Over Heels

Words & Music by Benny Andersson & Bjorn Ulvaeus

This 1981 Abba song dates from the days when their star was starting to fade a little. Even so, it revealed no decline in quality although it remains one of their less memorable single releases.

Hints & Tips: Watch the fingering in the right hand of this piece – you will need to practise this slowly. In the left hand take care with the notes C and C♯, which often use the same finger.

© Copyright 1981 Union Songs AB, Sweden. Bocu Music Limited for Great Britain and the Republic of Ireland.
All Rights Reserved. International Copyright Secured.

I Do, I Do, I Do, I Do, I Do

Words & Music by Benny Andersson & Bjorn Ulvaeus & Stig Anderson

The soaring close harmony saxophone riffs on this record recall the 1950s instrumentals of American bandleader Billy Vaughn as well as the closer-to-home sound of European Schlager music. An all-time Abba classic.

Hints & Tips: Play each group of two quavers in triplet rhythm – that is, make the first note twice as long as the second. This will give the piece a 'rolling' or 'swing' feel.

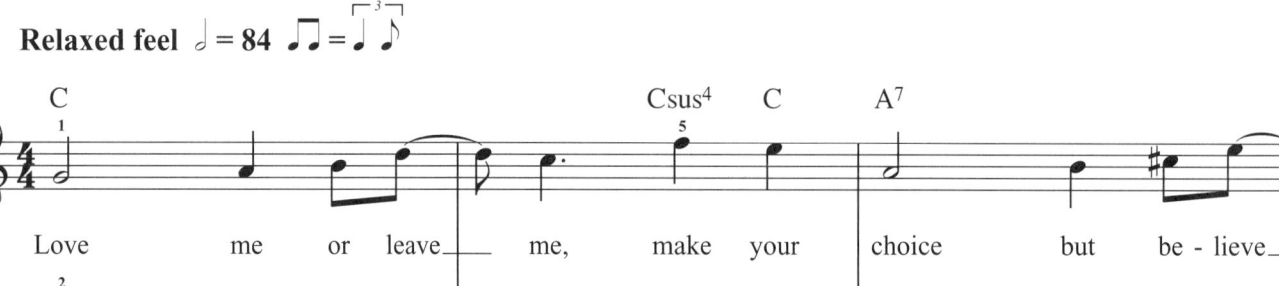

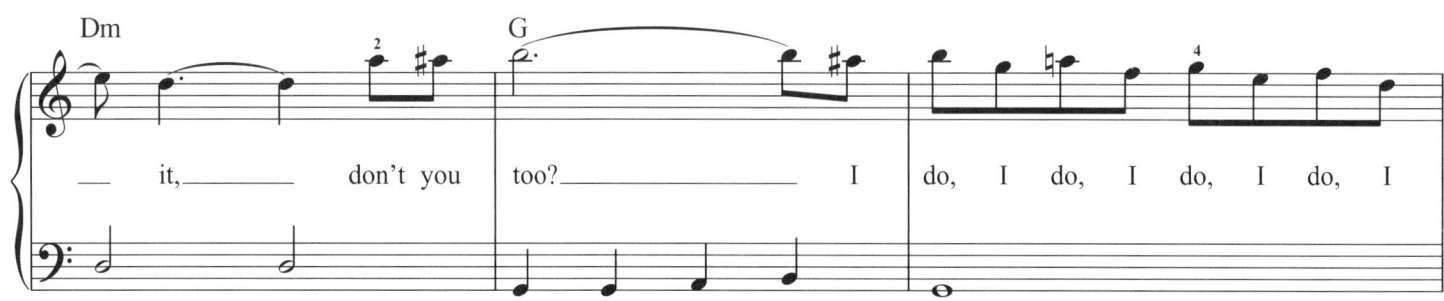

© Copyright 1975 Union Songs AB, Sweden. Bocu Music Limited for Great Britain and the Republic of Ireland.
All Rights Reserved. International Copyright Secured.

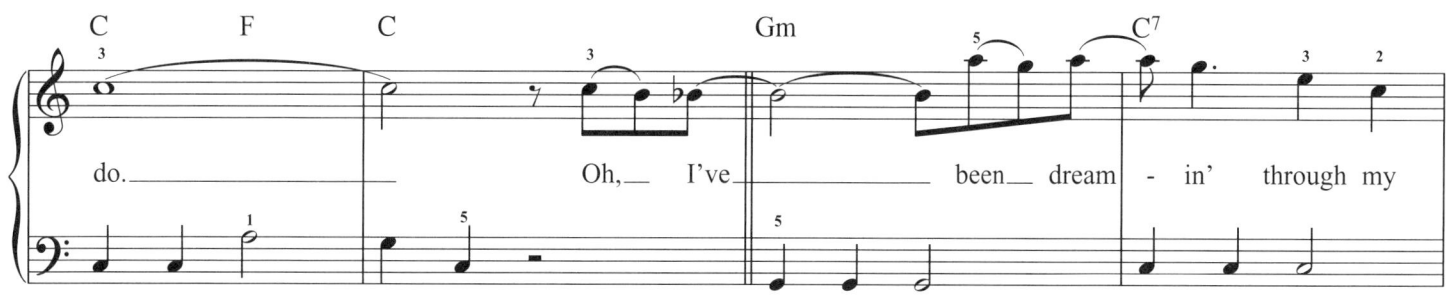
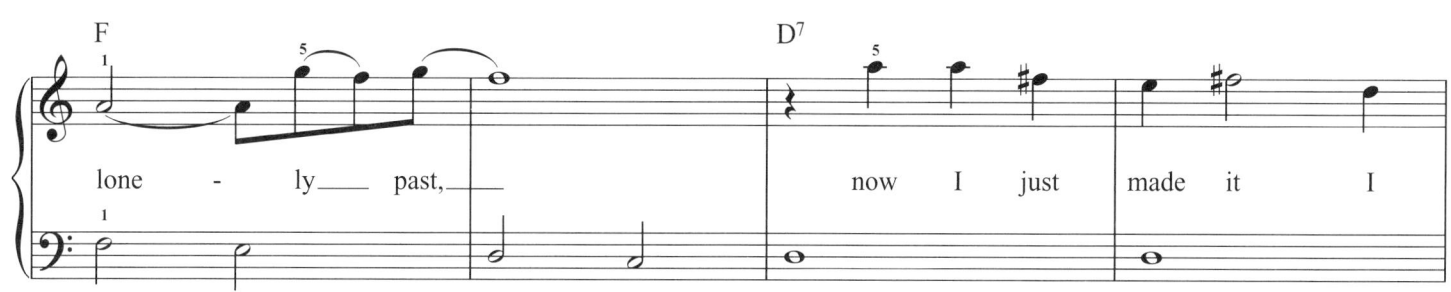
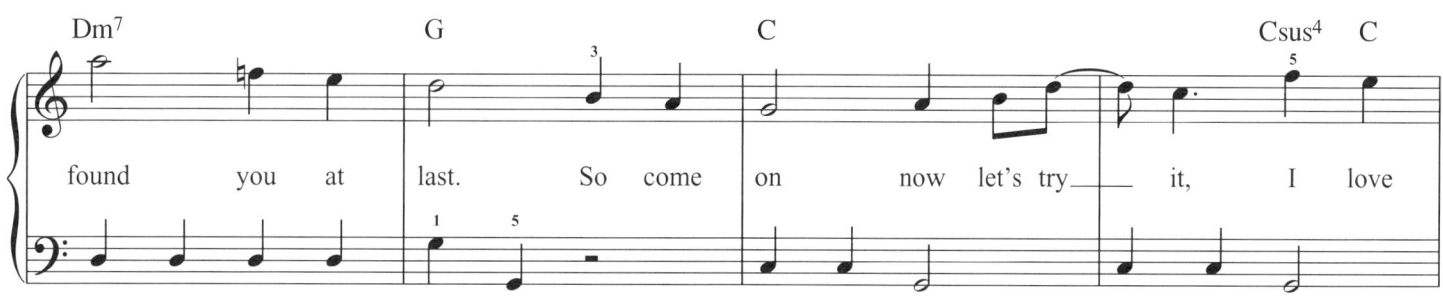
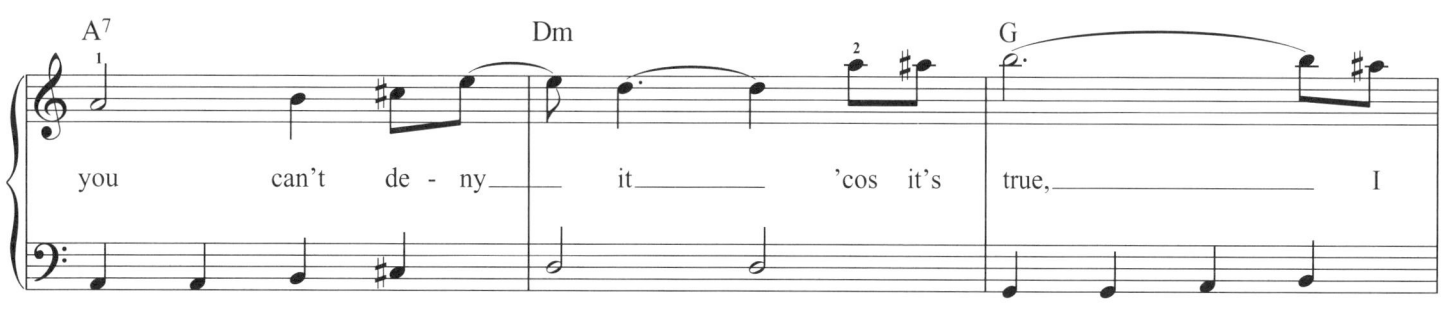
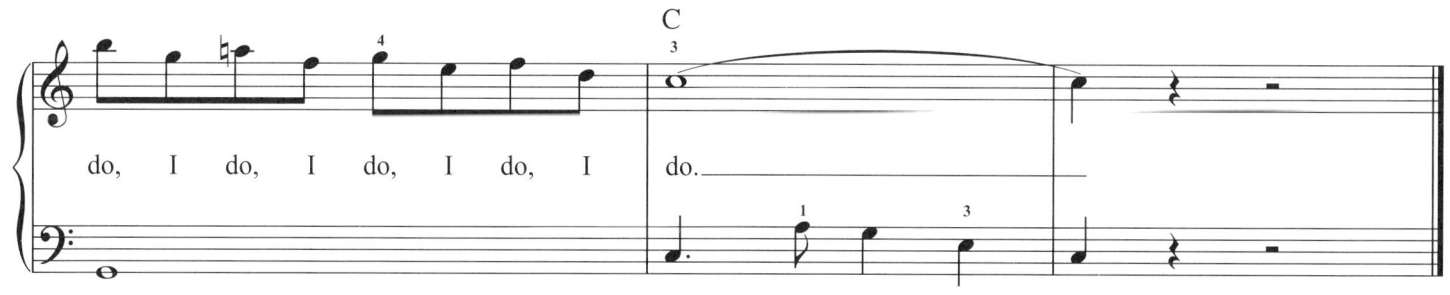

I Have A Dream

Words & Music by Benny Andersson & Bjorn Ulvaeus

A famous Abba anthem and one of their prettiest melodies, this song was probably written with the sole intention of creating a song which local children's choirs could join in with onstage.

Hints & Tips: Play the quavers in the left hand of this piece regularly and smoothly, following the fingering carefully. Don't miss the many dotted notes in the right hand.

© Copyright 1979 Union Songs AB, Sweden. Bocu Music Limited for Great Britain and the Republic of Ireland.
All Rights Reserved. International Copyright Secured.

Knowing Me, Knowing You

Words & Music by Benny Andersson & Bjorn Ulvaeus & Stig Anderson

Another Abba number that later became associated with a UK comedy show, 'Knowing Me, Knowing You' was the group's sixth consecutive No.1 hit in Germany and remains one of their best songs.

Hints & Tips: Notice that both hands play the same music at the beginning of this song. There's also a 2/4 bar to watch out for, and a fade at the end of the song.

Lay All Your Love On Me

Words & Music by Benny Andersson & Bjorn Ulvaeus

Released as a 12-inch single and backed with 'On And On And On', this song came out in 1981 and was aimed squarely at the dance circuit.

Hints & Tips: The left hand of this piece uses repeated crotchets almost throughout. Use these regular beats to help you play the right hand rhythms.

With movement ♩ = 132

I wasn't jealous before we met, now ev-'ry wom-an I

see is a pot-en-tial threat,

and I'm po-ses-sive, it is-n't nice, you've heard me say-ing that

smok-ing was my on-ly vice. But

© Copyright 1980 Union Songs AB, Sweden. Bocu Music Limited for Great Britain and the Republic of Ireland.
All Rights Reserved. International Copyright Secured.

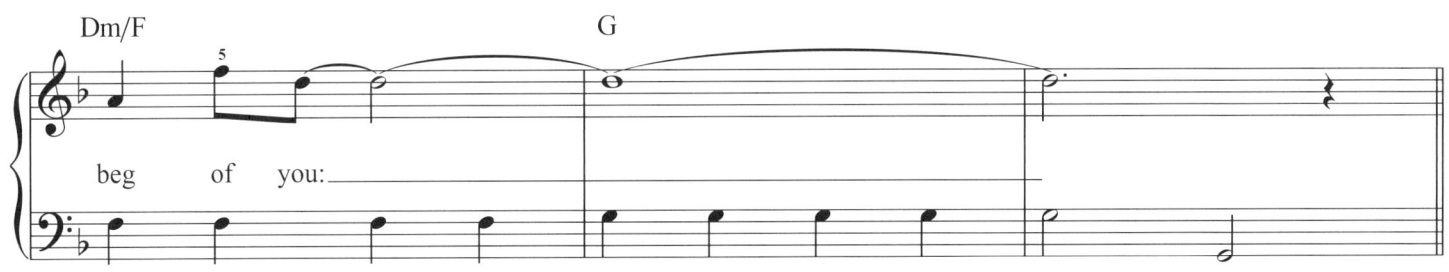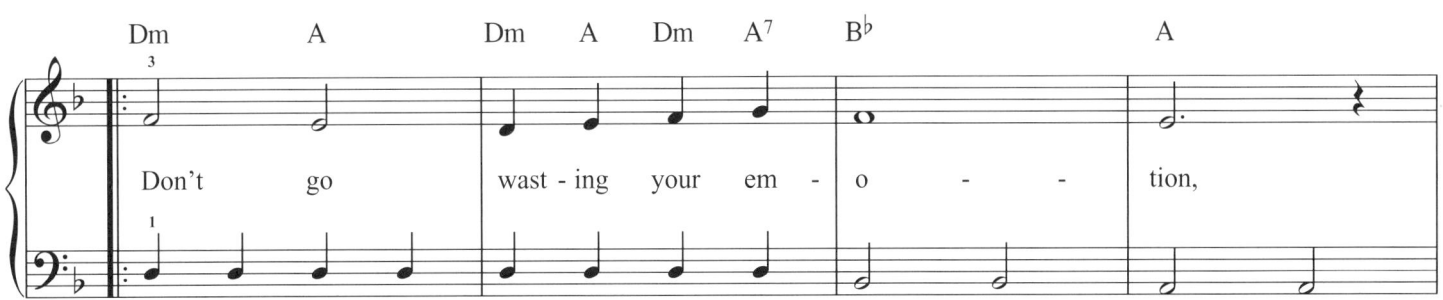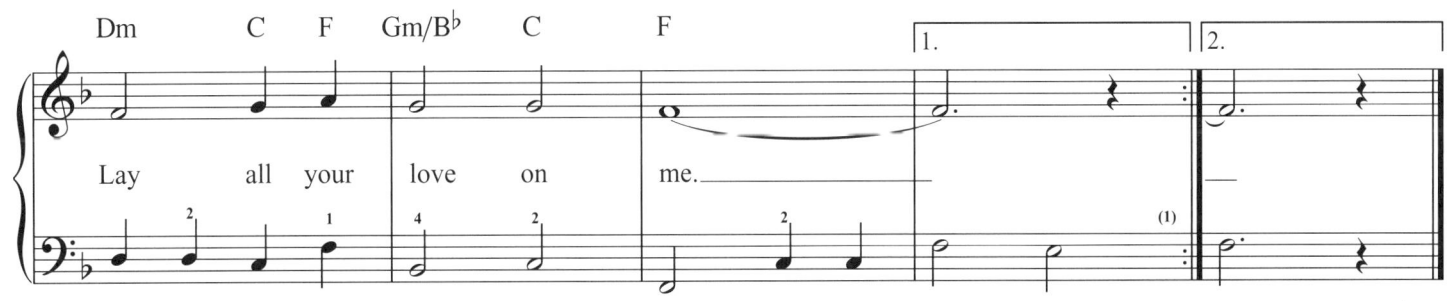

Mamma Mia

Words & Music by Benny Andersson & Bjorn Ulvaeus & Stig Anderson

The song that two decades later lent its name to the international smash Abba musical first came out in 1975. Anyone wanting to know what makes a great pop song need only listen to this sublime demonstration of how it is done.

Hints & Tips: Give extra practice time to the left hand chords in this piece. Practise them first by playing the bass note only, but be sure to use the correct finger. If you'd prefer, you can omit the upper notes of these chords.

© Copyright 1975 Union Songs AB, Sweden. Bocu Music Limited for Great Britain and the Republic of Ireland.
All Rights Reserved. International Copyright Secured.

Money, Money, Money

Words & Music by Benny Andersson & Bjorn Ulvaeus

Abba's fifth consecutive No.1 in Australia was another example of the ability of Andersson and Ulvaeus to hijack simple English phrases and turn them into hook-line chants with ridiculously catchy tunes.

Hints & Tips: The first four bars of this piece are repeated as the next four bars. In every piece of music you play, always look to see if there are any bars that repeat – this will save you practice time!

© Copyright 1976 Union Songs AB, Sweden. Bocu Music Limited for Great Britain and the Republic of Ireland.
All Rights Reserved. International Copyright Secured.

Fernando

Words & Music by Benny Andersson & Bjorn Ulvaeus & Stig Anderson

'Fernando' first appeared in a Swedish version called 'Tango' on a 1975 Anni-Frid Lyngstad solo album. With an English vocal overdub it became a 1976 hit under its more familiar title.

Hints & Tips: Play the minim-crotchet rhythm in the left hand of this song strongly, to give the music a bouncy dance feel.

The Name Of The Game

Words & Music by Benny Andersson & Bjorn Ulvaeus & Stig Anderson

This song takes us back to *ABBA: The Album* for which it was the very first track to be recorded back in 1977. As a single it subsequently made number one in both the UK and Ireland.

Hints & Tips: Give extra practice time to the bass part of this piece – especially the fingering in the opening eight bars. Don't miss the dotted notes in the melody.

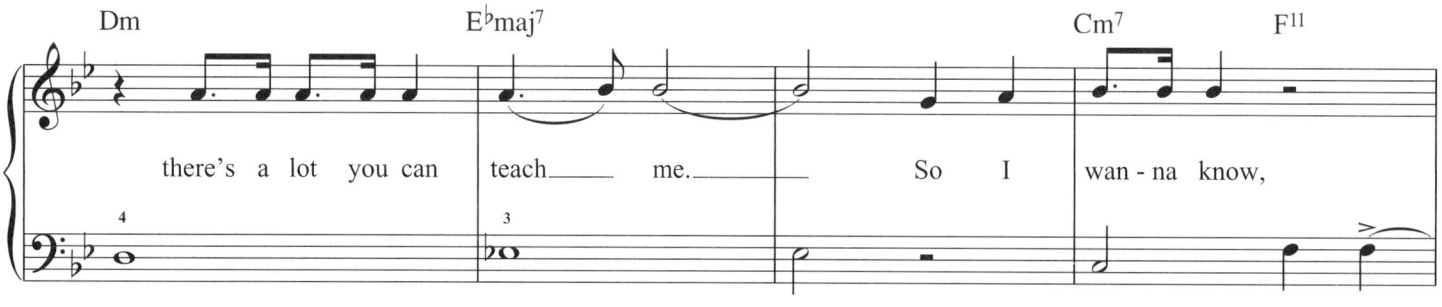

© Copyright 1977 Union Songs AB, Sweden. Bocu Music Limited for Great Britain and the Republic of Ireland.
All Rights Reserved. International Copyright Secured.

One Of Us

Words & Music by Benny Andersson & Bjorn Ulvaeus

Originally called 'Mi Amore', this wistful little song of regret dropped a broad hint to ABBA-watchers that by 1981 all was not well with their heroes' interpersonal relationships. Despite this it became the group's 13th No.1 hit in Ireland.

Hints & Tips: Take special care with the rhythms and time changes in this song. This piece will benefit from being played softly and legato (smoothly).

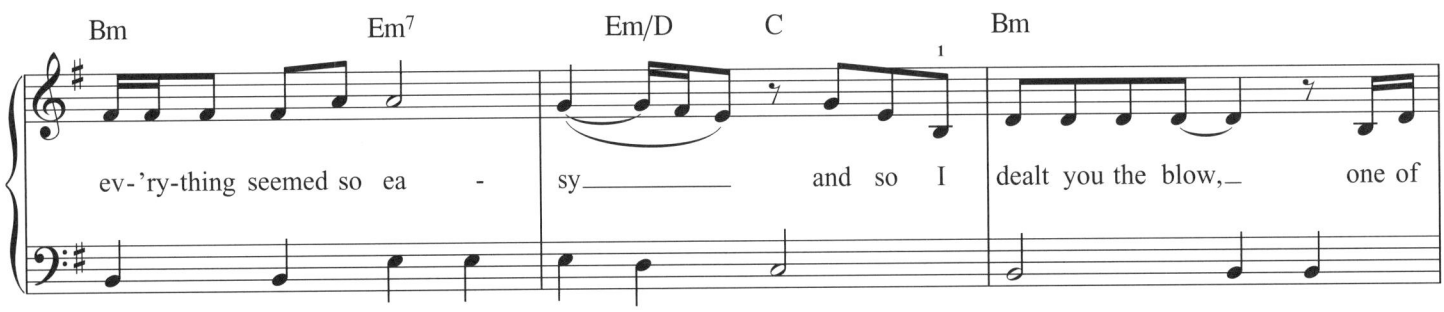
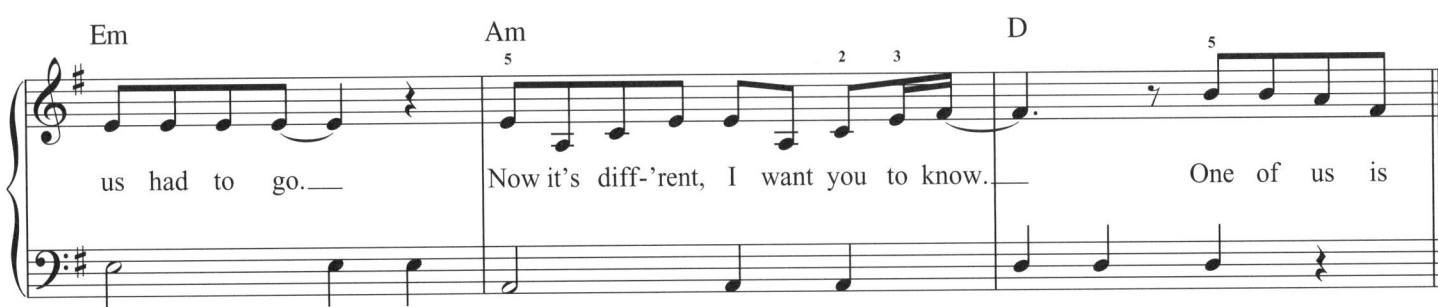

© Copyright 1981 Union Songs AB, Sweden. Bocu Music Limited for Great Britain and the Republic of Ireland.
All Rights Reserved. International Copyright Secured.

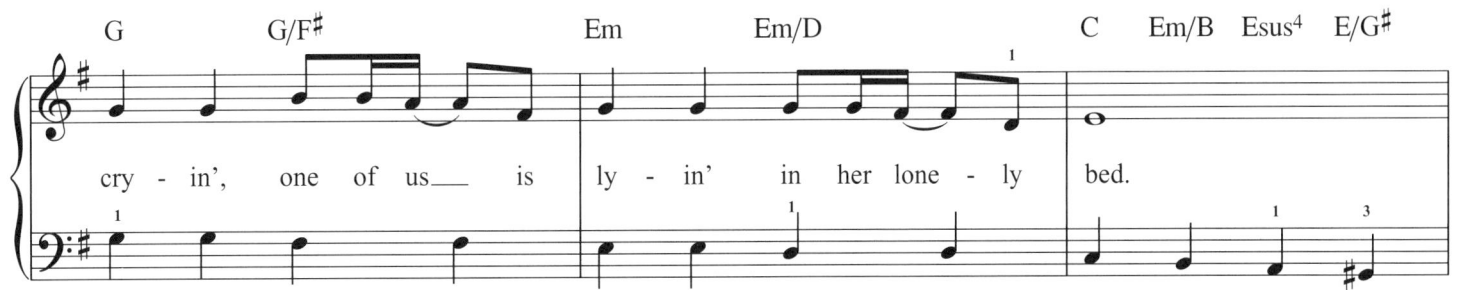

Ring Ring

Words & Music by Benny Andersson & Bjorn Ulvaeus, Stig Anderson, Neil Sedaka & Phil Cody

Along with 'Mamma Mia' and 'S.O.S.' this is one of the greatest Abba pop songs. The recording predated their Eurovision breakthrough – it was rejected by the Eurovision panel in 1973 and flopped upon its UK release. Influenced by Phil Spector's Wall of Sound and with English lyrics co-written by Neil Sedaka, it became an Abba favourite only belatedly.

Hints & Tips: You can play one hand only at the beginning of this piece, if you'd prefer – and do the same at the end. And always remember to practise slowly.

© Copyright 1973 Union Songs AB, Sweden. Bocu Music Limited for Great Britain and the Republic of Ireland.
All Rights Reserved. International Copyright Secured.

S.O.S.

Words & Music by Benny Andersson & Bjorn Ulvaeus & Stig Anderson

A major world-wide hit and the follow-up to Eurovision winner 'Waterloo', 'S.O.S.' was an instant Abba classic that welded another internationally recognisable slogan to a relentlessly catchy melody.

Hints & Tips: Follow the fingering carefully in the left hand, so as not to miss the wide stretches between the fingers. Notice that most phrases in the melody begin on the 'off-beat' – count the beats carefully so that you get this right.

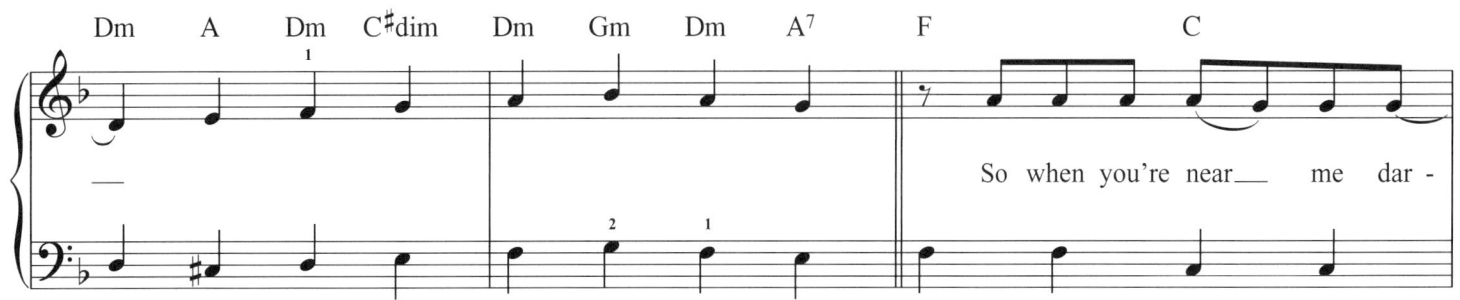

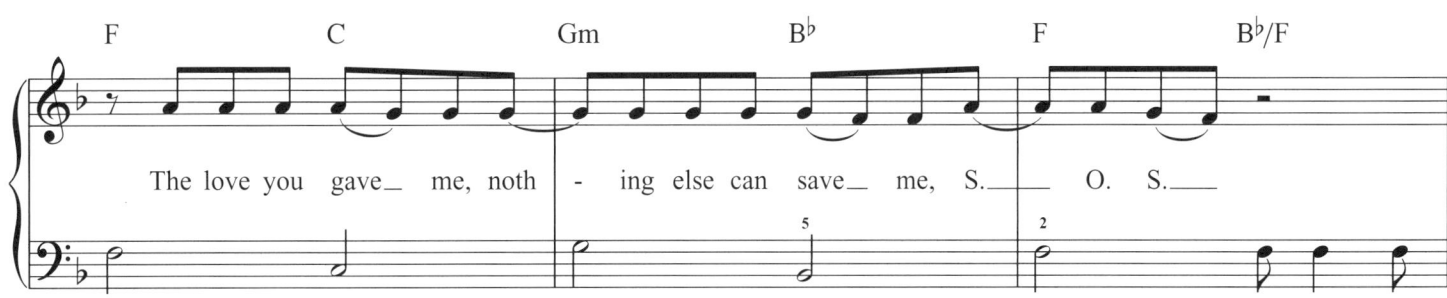
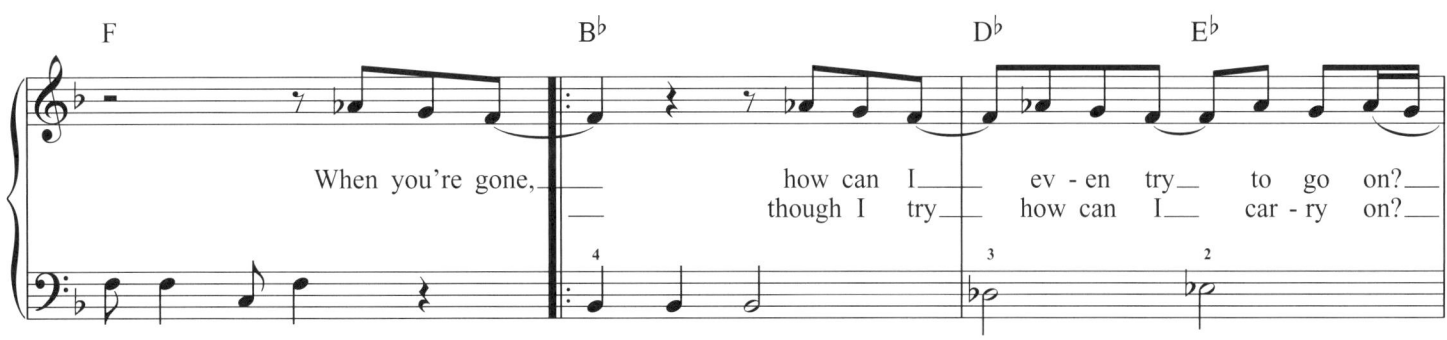

Summer Night City

Words & Music by Benny Andersson & Bjorn Ulvaeus

Originally intended for inclusion on the *Voulez-Vous* album, 'Summer Night City' was dropped and then edited down for release as the A-side of a single that reached No.1 in Sweden.

Hints & Tips: The bass of this piece repeats the same rhythm almost throughout. Keep these notes regular and rhythmic, to give the music a bouncy feel. Take care with the rhythm of the last two bars.

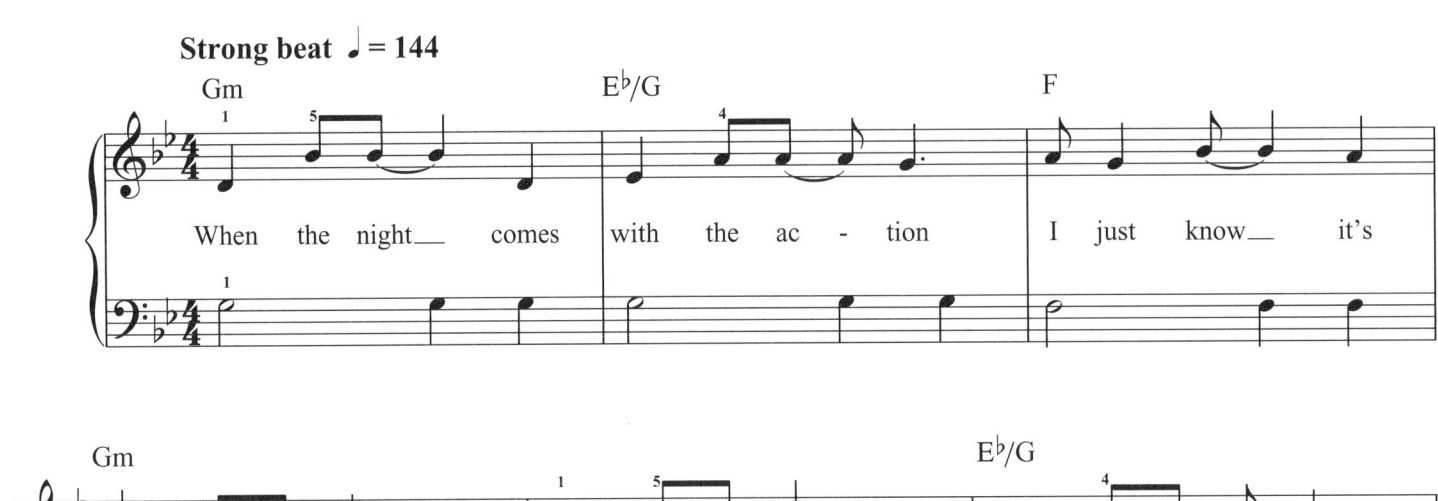

© Copyright 1978 Union Songs AB, Sweden. Bocu Music Limited for Great Britain and the Republic of Ireland.
All Rights Reserved. International Copyright Secured.

Super Trouper

Words & Music by Benny Andersson & Bjorn Ulvaeus

Abba's last British No.1 has the distinction of being the only song containing the word 'Glasgow' ever to top the UK charts. Another thumping anthem with a percussive lyric, it still has 'hit' written all over it.

Hints & Tips: Notice that the two halves of this piece are very similar. Always count a regular beat when you play music – this will help you play the correct rhythms.

© Copyright 1980 Union Songs AB, Sweden. Bocu Music Limited for Great Britain and the Republic of Ireland.
All Rights Reserved. International Copyright Secured.

Take A Chance On Me

Words & Music by Benny Andersson & Bjorn Ulvaeus

With its pounding off-beat and stuttering backing vocal, 'Take A Chance On Me' (1977) harks back to the urgency of the first Abba hits and was a big success in the United States. It was originally entitled 'Billy Boy' and the hit version came out of the second recording session attempt to cut it.

Hints & Tips: It is essential to 'count the beat' (four counts each bar) when you play this piece. Fit the rhythms of the right hand around the beat, as you play.

© Copyright 1977 Union Songs AB, Sweden. Bocu Music Limited for Great Britain and the Republic of Ireland.
All Rights Reserved. International Copyright Secured.

Thank You For The Music

Words & Music by Benny Andersson & Bjorn Ulvaeus

Andersson and Ulvaeus were already harbouring ambitions to write a musical long before *Chess*. This song, with its protracted solo vocal introduction, came from their 'mini-musical' *The Girl With The Golden Hair*.

Hints & Tips: Try and add a swing to the chorus ('Thank You For The Music...') of this song. Be sure to take extra care with the many accidentals in the piece.

© Copyright 1977 Union Songs AB, Sweden. Bocu Music Limited for Great Britain and the Republic of Ireland.
All Rights Reserved. International Copyright Secured.

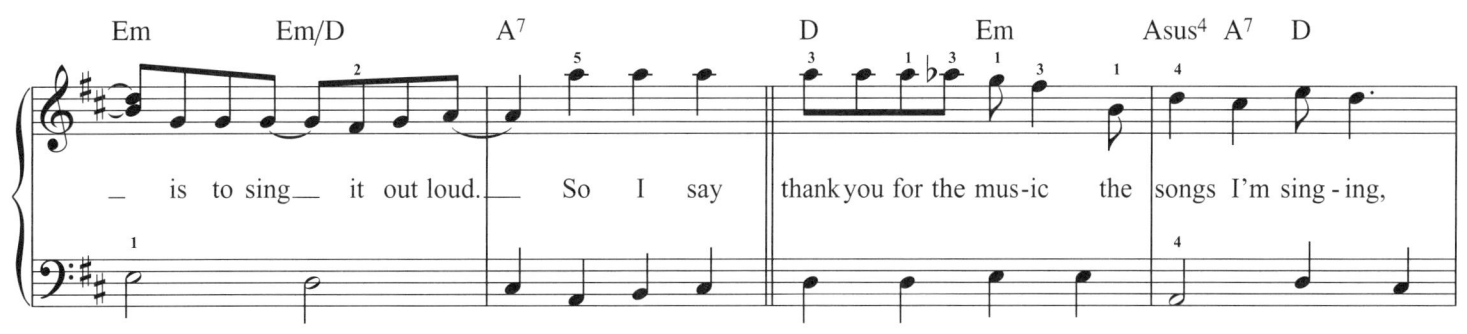

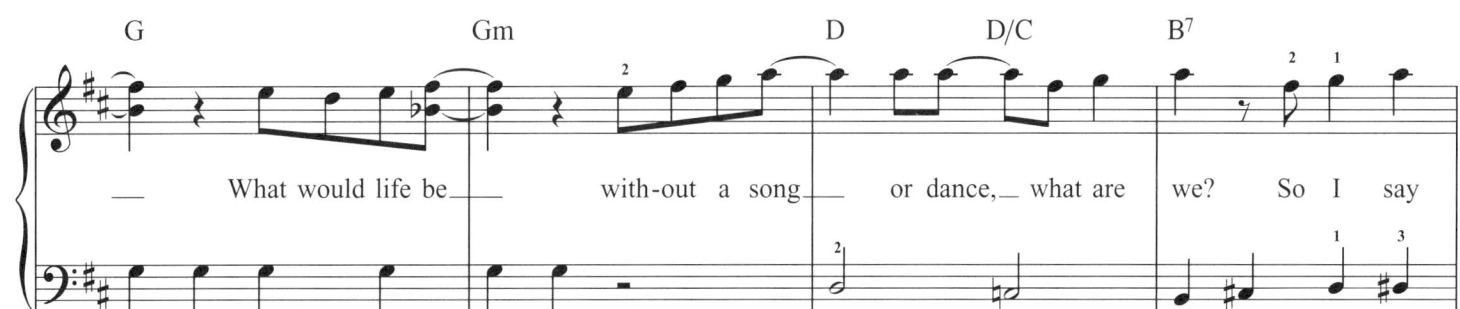

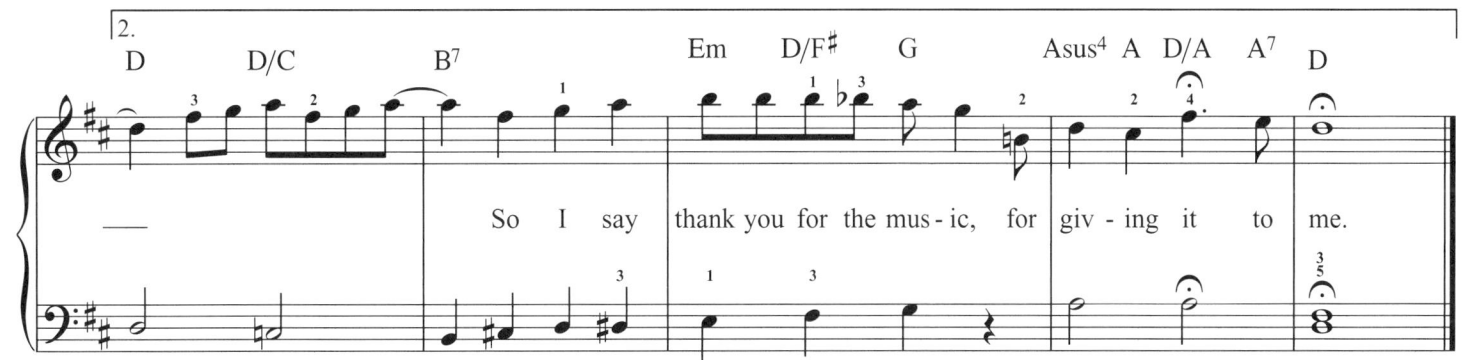

Waterloo

Words & Music by Benny Andersson & Bjorn Ulvaeus & Stig Anderson

The legendary breakout song with which four weirdly-dressed Swedes won The Eurovision Song Contest in Brighton, England in 1974. One critic said the hook line of 'Waterloo' stayed with you like a kick in the knee, but everyone else knew the song marked the start of something special.

Hints & Tips: Play the chorus of this song with a bright strong beat, taking care with the mixtures of dotted and non-dotted notes, which appear in both hands.

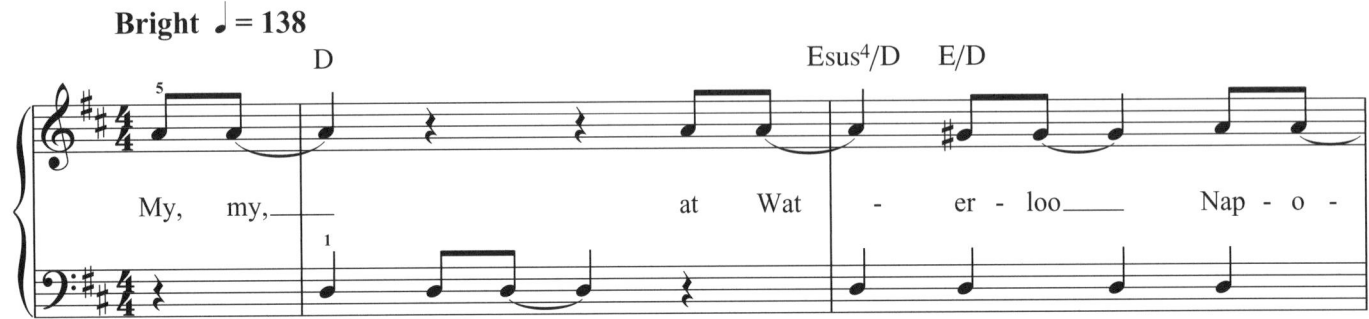

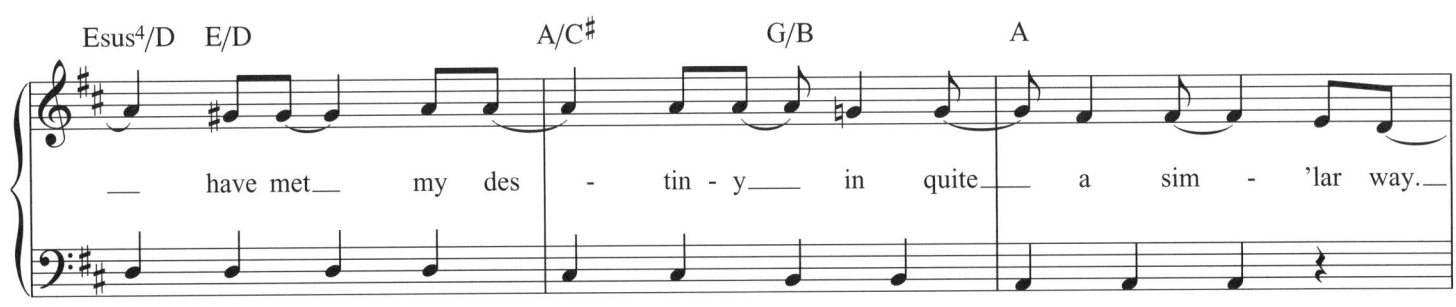

© Copyright 1974 Union Songs AB, Sweden. Bocu Music Limited for Great Britain and the Republic of Ireland.
All Rights Reserved. International Copyright Secured.

The Winner Takes It All

Words & Music by Benny Andersson & Bjorn Ulvaeus

Starting out with the title 'The Story Of My Life', this 1980 Abba song made No.1 in the UK and also reached the US Top Ten.

Hints & Tips: In the second part of the song, read the note names before the fingerings, in order not to be caught out by the wide stretches between the fingers.

Voulez-Vous

Words & Music by Benny Andersson & Bjorn Ulvaeus

Unusually, this memorable Abba hit was partly recorded in the United States, at Criteria Studios in Miami. The song had been written in the Bahamas and the group decided to record the backing track in nearby Florida with members of the disco group Foxy making a contribution.

Hints & Tips: This piece calls for a disco feel. Playing the bass notes (especially the accented notes) strongly, will help you to achieve this. Count the beat carefully, so as not to miss the rests at the beginning of some bars in the melody.

© Copyright 1979 Union Songs AB, Sweden. Bocu Music Limited for Great Britain and the Republic of Ireland.
All Rights Reserved. International Copyright Secured.